LITTLE BLACK BOOK

ASKING FOR MONEY

ALLISON MCENTEE

Little Black Book: Asking for Money
Copyright © 2019 by Allison McEntee

ISBN (Print): 978-1-54398-492-7

What is this book?

This book was not written for you to devote hours and hours to reading.
Please do not do that. No one has time for that.
After all, to quote a past manager of mine, "Time is money!"

This little black book is a tactical, hands-on "how to" resource in asking people for money. It was originally written from my personal experience in advertising sales, but in the midst of writing it, I found it to be useful across many different sectors and colleagues. For example, my influencer friends wanted to learn how to best represent their personal brands and unlock bigger dollars from brands, and my neighbors trying to drive higher fundraising donations also found it useful. Younger executives also dove into the book when asking for a raise, or asking for more with a new job prospect.

Either way, what I learned is that everyone has to ask for money at some point and in some capacity, and it ranks up there with public speaking for most. It's terrifying, it's not fun, it's awkward, and most people hate to do it.

Treat this little black book as your insider's guide to asking for what you want, and what you deserve.

Feel free to read it cover to cover, but it is best suited for when you really need to dive in and focus on one particular area. For example,

- Use it as a tool to prep for a meeting, ensuring you are covering all areas of potential discussion with a client/buyer/boss (someone who holds the purse strings and has decision making power)
- Use it as a reference guide for asking the right questions when "checking in" on the status of a potential partnership or pay increase. The questions will help you gain more intel on the status of your deal or opportunity at play

Either way, this little black book is your quick, no bullshit guide in asking for money.

Work from it, reference it and use it as a tool to get you what you want.

Contents

Your Job:
Understanding your role and purpose

If you are asking for money. You are selling something. It could be a product, it could be your personal brand, it could be anything.

And a sales person's #1 job is to produce. Produce money. That's it.

When people ask me, "What do you do for a living?" I jokingly, but truthfully say, "I harass people for money." It always gets a chuckle, but it's true. My job is to navigate a piece of business to find money to support the product/brand/start-up I represent, then to ask/harass people for that money.

When you sell, there is no glory. It's your job. It's what you get paid to do.

What is celebrated is the journey (everyone loves a "journey," am I right?) that you took to get there – the road you had to create and navigate, the window-in you had to find to break into an account, the people you met and turned into advocates or moles, the way you asked the right questions to give you intel to take you to the next conversation…*those* are the things we celebrate.

True salespeople are driven by one thing, and one thing only – money.

That is it. Plain and simple.

When I hire new salespeople, or someone expresses to me their interest in going into sales, I ask them just one question, "What drives you?" If they don't say "money" instantaneously, they are not killers. They may be good, but they're not going to change my business.

Within a sales organization, at most you'll have about 1 or 2 **true salespeople.** At most.
Sure, there are some good sellers that like a "nice work environment," or like to "represent a company or product they believe in," but at the end of the day, if money is not their #1 driver, they are not going to be a top producer. And that's okay...it takes all kinds to build a business.

This brings me to **activity**.
Sales is self-inflicted pain. If you want to make money, you apply pressure to yourself. No one pushes you, you push yourself. If you want to make money, you create activity. If you do not have meetings, calls, or you are not traveling to meet clients, etc. you are not selling. Sitting on your butt and cold emailing counts, but it's minimal and you'll see pennies. It's not going to drive big business.
Activity = Selling.

All You Need: Just three (3) things.

A past manager once told me, "our business is a C level business. If you got Cs in school, you'll succeed. No doubt. If you got As, well, you'll either really succeed/dominate or get bored as hell and leave." Sales is not for intellects. It is for every day, street-smart folks...those that know how to create connections with people, listen to needs/pain points and deliver solutions for their partners. They understand the "sell me this pen" trick and master it.

What's really fun about sales is the fact that you can actually make more money than your higher-educated, debt-ridden lawyer/doctor/therapist neighbors. And honestly, I'm not even sure college is a must to be stellar at this gig. The undergrad diploma is just something you need to get started. At least right now...who knows what the next ten years will bring.

There are only three (3) things you need to be good at, to be good in sales.

#1 - Be Organized

And I mean, really organized.
For example, take a look at your wallet.... go, now...take a look. Does everything have a place? Are your bills stacked highest to lowest, cards in designated spots? Or are there receipts and gum wrappers sticking out? I can tell you right now, if your own wallet isn't organized, how are you going to be on top of your game when it comes to selling something to someone?

Again, sales is self-inflicted pain, so the more you are buttoned up, organized, well-prepped for meetings, and on top of your follow ups, all will fall into place.

And when I say organized, I mean:
- Client Outreach - remembering when you last connected, leveraging your knowledge from your previous meetings (personal and professional) to take your conversation to the next level.
- Personal Details - any personal "details" that a client shares (she is getting married next year, expecting a baby, grew up in Cleveland, gluten-free), all of it…write it down, and under their name (make an excel). We will dive into this a bit more later in the book, but these "details" are immensely helpful and show your attention to your client, which in turns elevates their confidence in you to take care of them.
- Book a Meeting – location is confirmed, you are not late (being on time is late), call-in numbers are included in the invite, and time zones are reflected correctly (note, if your client is in a different time zone than you, don't send them an email with options in your time zone – think of them first, this is customer service at its core).
- Prep for the Meeting – we will dive deep into this subject later in the book, but preparing for a meeting should take place days, even the week prior to the meeting. You want to be thorough, thoughtful and you want to have ideas and questions at the ready. If you do not prepare, you will not sell. There's nothing wrong with over-prepping.
- Send a Reminder – the day before the meeting, send an email reminder to the client – a super quick one. Something like, "Hi Erica, Excited to catch up with you at 10am tomorrow at your office. Have a great night!" With these reminders, be careful, as you are not asking to confirm the meeting again (stay away from, "I hope we're still on," or "does 10am still work for you?" These are just easy ways for them to get out of the meeting. Just state your enthusiasm and confirm the logistical details. Also, send this reminder the afternoon prior to the day of your meeting.

Not at 11pm the night prior, or days prior. Put yourself in the client's shoes and think about what's easiest for them.

- Update Your Manager – I'm sure you've shared your overall activity schedule with your manager prior to the meeting, but what is equally or even more important is that they want to see the outcome. After every meeting, get in the rhythm of writing a quick Call Report. Nothing fancy, nothing wild here – just a digital "dump" of all of the information you gathered and in a bulleted, easy-to-digest form. Also, the benefits of doing this right after you get out of the meeting, you retain more details. I typically write notes in meetings on a notebook, then I take those notes and rip them out of the notebook and throw them out after they are in digital form. I use this format (below) and save it in a Google Doc, so I can always refer back (when I am prepping for the next meeting).

Date/Client Name/Role

Purpose
- xxx

Notes
- xxx

Next Steps
- xxx

- Update Your Split Partner – we will dive deep into this topic later in the book as well (and it may not be relevant to you if you're a local fundraiser), but being organized also stems into providing intel and insights to your split partners. In case anyone is unsure what a split partner is, it's your counterpart at work that shares the account with you. Perhaps for geographic reasons, or for category reasons. You need to act like you have the "same brain" and leverage what you learn from each other to move down the tunnel to winning business. So, after a meeting, write your Call Report, and CC your split partner when you email it to management.

Being highly organized is a skill. The more organized and buttoned-up you are, the more confident and "smooth and carefree" you are perceived. When you're prepared, your clients will want to work with you. They will believe you will employ the same attention to detail toward their business.

If you mess up with any of these areas noted (even if it's a small detail, like showing up without confirming for a meeting), it shows you're not on your game. The details matter, and clients (and your managers) are watching.

#2 - Be Able to Talk with People

Sounds simple, doesn't it?
Well, in sales, you have to be able to not only talk with people in a large group setting, but also host one-on-one time with C-Suites, and decision makers. You've got to hold your own, lead the conversation, and be perceived as someone they want to work with (professionally and personally). You have to be able to persuade in either scenario (large or small settings), and you also have to find a way to make a connection with all individuals.

I have pitched to rooms of 50+ people that wished they were someplace else. I have also had to carry a conversation for over an hour with a 70-year-old executive over lunch – I mean, what do we have in common??

This all takes practice and even those that are "born for sales" have to work at it, and we all get better at it each time we practice.

One tip I can tell you…especially when it comes to the C-Suite, as their interests are less on the tactical, and more on the "really getting to know you" path. I once sat down with a CMO of a global travel company, and her first question was, "tell me about yourself." She was not interested in the company I was representing (at least at first), as she was more interested in getting to know who I was personally, my background and my intent. She turned into a mentor of mine, and a year later, I asked her about that opening question..." tell me about yourself" ...how that is not a common opener (at least for me). She said she asks that of everyone she meets with and finds it to be quite telling with people's different responses. She says the right response is, "what would you like to know?" To put it back on her, and let her take the lead with the conversation. Very interesting. How would have you responded?

#3 – Ride the Rollercoaster

This is the toughest part about sales.
This business is a rollercoaster. Some say it's a "wave"...up and down.

You have to be able to "ride the wave" and move with the highs and the lows. If you can't master this one, I'd suggest you move to another line of work. Seriously.

For example, you could be working on a deal for a year and all signs point to YES. You have met with everyone that touches the business (associates to VPs, and across all partners), you've worked through rounds and rounds of plan revisions, and you've traveled across the country so much that you begin to make friends with the flight crews. Then, out of the blue...you get the call. The break up call, where they tell you the deal is dead. Perhaps for a reason out of your control - budgets change, management changes, natural disasters happen, you name it. I've heard it all. I always say, "there are 80 ways a deal can fall apart."

You've got to ride the rollercoaster and pick yourself up, put a smile on your face, and thank the client for the consideration and the experience. There *will* be a next time and you want to be considered as a partner that is supportive and genuinely wants to work with them. Plus, people change jobs all the time. One client that loved you at Company X could bring that same enthusiasm for you when they move to Company Y.

Once you get that "break up phone call" and you start complaining, whining, or even turn angry, they will never give you another opportunity to pitch. You have to hold your head up high, thank them for the experience, and move onto the next. There are so many options for buyers these days, so if you are a pain to deal with, they will take their money someplace else.

And then on the flip side, when the wave is high and you are closing deals and having some great momentum, do not be an asshole to your internal team. Be a coach, share your learnings, and leverage your intel with the team. Be humble and know that this job you've got is a rollercoaster, and a new wave is coming your way soon.

#1 Rule of Sales: Stop Talking

There is really one rule I like to stick to when it comes to selling. Just stop talking.

Listening to a client is the most important thing you can do. Again, listening to a client is the most important thing you can do.

Did you hear that? Stop and think about it.

A *successful meeting* looks like this:
<u>30 Minutes Total</u>
- The first 25 minutes - you are asking questions, you are listening, you are gaining intel on what they like, not like, their hopes, their interests, their challenges, etc.
- Then, the last 5 minutes – you tell them about your product and how it delivers on what they want. You literally tee-up your pitch to deliver exactly against what they expressed interest/needs in.

Even if a client wants to hear about your offering first, you can give a little taste, perhaps a quick 411, but then bring it right back to them, and dig deep into what they need for their business.

You will not be able to sell anything unless you truly know what the client needs/wants. And no client wants to just hear about you and your company.

The Right Questions: Finding Intel

Some clients will tell you exactly what they think of you, your idea, and your offering. You will know quickly if these clients want to buy your product or not. It is actually fantastic…to know exactly where you stand with a client. While other clients, you've got to really dig-in, ask the right questions, and determine how far along you *really* are in the consideration funnel.

For example, you have submitted a proposal, and it's been a week. Sending a "checking in" email to a client, will do nothing for you. It is easily deleted as there is no action requested or no benefit provided to them.

Instead, submit a proposal and tell them when you will be checking in on their initial feedback. Tell them your schedule on gaining feedback.

And when you do send that "checking in" email, ask the right questions. Here are some to think through:
Any initial/knee jerk reactions to our idea?
What did you think of our idea? Like/love/hate?
Anything we can do to tweak the plan to get this to a place you can't wait to share with your client?
What's your timing on sharing your recommendation with the client?

With any email you send to a prospective buyer, you must always send some sort of value. Never just ask questions/ask for updates, but instead, share new intel, new product launches, new performance reports, etc. – every communication you provide to a client should have value back for them. You could even do a simple google search and see what they've been up to press-wise. Send it to them, show them you see what their up to and that you are in-tune with their business.

Typically, no response from a buyer = not good.
Sales is like dating - when someone likes you, you know it.
If a client wants to buy you (and your product), you know it.

Another time to ask for intel is when you get the RFP (Request For Proposal). You need to determine where you stand in their consideration and how to submit the best program. Get in the habit of asking, "Why did you send this to us? How come we are among your consideration?" It may sound ridiculous to ask these things (and you can even point out how ridiculous it may sound in asking), but the answers will tell you two (2) things:

1) Maybe there is something specific they want to see in the submission. Maybe you are on the consideration list for a specific reason. You will want to know what this is and deliver it as part of your submission.

2) If they do not answer or cannot answer why you were given the RFP, then you are not a strong contender. Again, it goes back to…if they really want you, they will tell you…you will know. And knowing you are not a true contender is as valuable as finding out you are. Gaining intel here is the most valuable part. And being able to track and report projections appropriately to internal management is crucial. For those prospects that do not provide you clear direction, still submit your strongest effort, but perhaps be more hesitant in its strength as a valid deal in your pipeline. Your management will thank you (and trust you).

Being able to hop on a quick call with the buyer once you receive the RFP is also extremely helpful. Do not use this precious time for them to walk you through the RFP (you can read it on your time, and please (!!!) read BEFORE you get on a call with them), but instead use this time to really dig in and find out how you can win the business. If you cannot get on the phone with them, look back to your Call Reports, and confirm back the needs they shared with you prior to gaining the

RFP. Ensure you are up to speed on their KPIs, business challenges and expectations as a partner.

If you are a lucky duck and can get on the phone with them or meet in person, here is where a casual conversation can help you. Try and navigate more on your ability to win the business.

Ask questions, such as:
How many other potential partners were RFPd? Are we 1 of 50? Or one of 3? Is this a jump-ball/one winner-takes-all sort of approach, or are you looking to work with a handful of partners? Is there a particular purpose you're looking to fulfill in working with me (as part of a grander campaign approach?)

Knowing your competition and what you're up against will help you navigate your points of differentiation and define how you should position your pitch to stand out among the submissions. Sometimes buyers will not tell you these answers, but depending on your relationship and approach, they may. NOTE – do not ask these questions in an email, or in a group setting. These sorts of insights are only given when the buyer feels comfortable and wants to truly help you create the best submission possible. And most likely, no one will give you these answers in writing.

Also...
Call out...any battles or areas we'll need to address? Anything we can help provide in squashing any doubt in our offering/our product? Anything we need to correct from prior experience working together?

Knowing where there may be any doubts or knowing what areas you will need to further explain, will help your client gain confidence in your offering. No one product/property is perfect, so you'll need to know where the soft spots are.

Your goal with your submission is to:
1) Get the idea right – something with a hook and makes sense for their campaign needs/objectives...something they get excited about.

2) Share a contract/plan they can't say no to – ensure its competitive and makes them look good to their management

3) Provide "ammo" to the buyer so they are confident and proud to recommend your program. Making their job easy is the way to go – answer their questions timely and be comprehensive.

The Meeting:
Three (3) Parts to a Meeting with a Buyer

For any meeting, in-person or on the phone, there are three (3) parts.

Part #1 – Prepare for the Meeting

If you walk into a meeting, or host a conference call with a buyer, and you have not prepped, you will not win their business. Period.

The smart clients will know if you've prepared for the visit. So, be ready.
It's not just learning about their business, but it is also preparing for how you are going to lead the time together – and your ultimate goal for the meeting. The strategy is as important as the information you gather and the questions you ask.

For any meeting (it's your first, or it's your 5th, or perhaps it's even with an existing buyer), I have a "Meeting Checklist" document I complete (next page). Get in the rhythm of answering these questions before each meeting. Spend time here (30min max…again, time is money!), really dive in, understand your client and begin to put together your framework for the meeting.

And when to prep for a meeting? Do it on Friday, as you prepare for your week ahead. Perhaps even do it first-thing Friday morning (7am/8am). Not many people want to receive an email from a sales rep early AM on a Friday (more on email strategy later in this book), so the early Friday AM time slot is devoted to you to prep for the week ahead. You'll want to head into Monday with everything done and ready.

Do not waste 9-5p prime time working hours for prep work (or "getting your expenses done" work). Do these things on off hours.

Meetings/Calls can come up within the week and on short notice, but no matter what, prep.

The Meeting Checklist:

Items to Know BEFORE the Meeting about your prospective buyer/client:

- Their Facebook (# Followers, what sorts of content are they posting?)
- Their Insta (# Followers, what are they posting?)
- Their Twitter (# Followers, what are they posting?)
- MediaRadar/Winmo (Competitive Set, Creative, Perfect Pitch)
- SellerCrowd (what's the 411 in the business?)
- Your Property (have we posted anything about them? If positive, show)
- Their Website (what are they promoting?)
- Any Press on them? Google it.
- Have we pitched them before? Bring the pitch and know why we didn't make the plan.
- Have we worked with the client before? Good/bad learnings?
- Have we worked with the agency before? If so, what accts. Be ready to share.
- Have we worked with the brand's competitors? Be ready to show the work.
- Have we worked in the category? Be ready to show the work.

Meeting Attendees (also, see if you have anything in common with them):

- Name
- Title
- # of Years Experience
- Education
- Any fun facts? FB, Insta, etc. Don't be a crazy stalker, but you know what I mean…
- Determine/Predict the decisions makers (and star their name, so you know who to look out for)

Questions to Ask in the Meeting:

- Target Audience?
- Timing for their initiative?
- Planning Cycle - when/if will they RFP?
- Goal of the program?
- Any performance goals/needs to note? KPIs?
- What's the most important factor? Reach, content, activation?
- When it comes to content, what do they dig most? Video, articles, influencers, etc?
- Proud Partners they want to share? And why?
- Do they have a dream program? Anything personally they'd love to do?
- Any battles they see off the bat with your product? Anything that we'll need to combat right away? Any pain points?

Always bring ideas.
Just to have in your back pocket, nothing formal here.
Throw them out to get a sense of what the buyer likes/dislikes.

Identify your goal for the meeting.
Do you want an RFP, do you want another meeting with more team members?
What are you looking to achieve from the meeting?

Part #2 – The Meeting

Today is the day – you have your meeting scheduled.
You have already sent your "confirmation email" and you have prepped.

If in person, show up 10/15minutes prior to the meeting.
If calling in, call in 3 minutes prior to the start of the call.

Never leave a client waiting for you. If there's any waiting at all, it is you waiting for them.
As you are sitting in the lobby waiting to go in, or listening to hold music on the conference line, refer back to your completed "Meeting Checklist." Refresh your brain, so it is top of mind and a quick reference.

Next, you are greeted to start the meeting, or they chime into the call. *"Hi there! So great to meet you!"*

In the first 3 seconds, they will judge you – in person and on the phone. You will be judged. Get used to it and have fun with it! Smile, be enthusiastic, look good, and be a pleasant person. I am not telling you to be inauthentic, I'm just saying don't yawn, don't complain about your day, don't remark about the weather (NEVER talk about the weather), traffic, etc…come in excited to share time with them.

Quick Tip, never say…*"thank you so much for taking time out of your day to meet with me."* Probably the worst thing you could ever say. If you say this, you are already positioning yourself as the inferior one in the dialogue. You are equals – so, instead say, "So great to meet you. Happy we could get together!"

And another Quick Tip – try not to book meetings back-to-back. After the meeting, allow time for you to complete/send a Call Report, travel to your next meeting (get there early) and refresh your brain for the next meeting.

You are the leader of the meeting, you control the dialogue, the pace, the conversation, the questions. You are also the keeper of the time.

Most meetings are 30 minutes, some shorter, some longer, it varies, but regardless, clients have limited time to spend with a vendor, so right from the start of the meeting, confirm with them the end time. Ask, *"do we have a hard stop at 10am?"* Note it, and go. You are the one that will control the flow of the meeting and you are the one that will end the meeting. Trust me, they will appreciate your acknowledgment of their needs and see you as responsible/thoughtful potential partner.

And just a reminder, (as this is the most important rule in sales), a *successful meeting* looks like this:
30 Minutes Total
- The first 25 minutes - you are asking questions, you are listening, you are gaining intel on what they like, not like, their hopes, their interests, their challenges, etc.
- Then, the last 5 minutes – you tell them about your product and how it delivers on what they want.

Within the meeting (and this could take place over the course of several meetings), there are three (3) key people you need to identify and "win over."
1) **The Decision Maker** – title is not always indicative here so beware, but as you ask questions/navigate conversations, you will see them appear
2) **The Advocate** - the person that loves your product more than anyone else and will go-to-bat for it among the team and with the client. They are also your mole and will give you insider intel. Stay tight with them.
3) **The Hater** - oh you'll see this person immediately. They're my favorite. They're skeptical, their arms are crossed, and maybe they're not even paying attention. They are crucial to winning over, as their "no" could be detrimental to winning. A deal can fall apart if just one person says no.

Along with identifying the people in the room, your job is to also "read the room" and access your materials. Simply put, the higher the title of the client, the less stuff you'll take out of your bag. A manager once told me, "executives don't take notes." Executives want great/heady conversations. They don't want you to write down their dialogue.

So, if I'm with a CMO, it's a discussion. That said, I will bring out my notebook when they are giving me names of people on their team to talk to (as next steps), or specific action items to follow up on, etc.

If I'm not with a C-Suite, I bring out my notepad + pen immediately.

My notebook is what includes the "Meeting Checklist" highlights and helps me structure/guide the conversation. I treat it as my "meeting workflow," referencing work they've created with other publishers, questions I have for them, ideas to share with them, etc.

Do not host a meeting and bury your head in your notebook writing extensive notes. I've sadly seen this happen. It's robotic and not natural to a conversation. The notebook serves purely as a reference guide and place for you to quickly jot down highlights/needs. I'll share more on what you do with these "notes" post meeting found later in this workbook.

Your Laptop.
The laptop comes into play, when and only when:
1) You're showing work to a client (ensure your hotspot is live and ready prior to the meeting…also something you can do in the lobby as you want to go in, and be sure you already own every dongle imaginable so you're ready no matter the office set up)
2) You've been asked to share a visual/overview of your property (again, you're not doing this until you've heard about their business needs, asked questions, etc). Even in large lunch/learns where the purpose is for you to introduce your property to a room of 30 clients, ask questions first, figure out what brands/products are represented in the room, what they are most interested in buying these days, what's working and what's not, etc.

If you start your meeting with showing a deck, you've lost.

So many issues with this move. #1) you failed the 25/5-minute structure, and #2) you've created a more formal meeting experience, which in turn will not give you the juicy intel you need to really dive in and win the business.

In-person meetings can also take place in non-office environments, such as lunches, coffees, baseball games, etc. Casual is good and can yield fantastic intel findings. Plus, people give money to people they like, so a more casual experience lets everyone's guard down (at least more so than in an office). Do not bring out your laptop at a casual meeting.

Real story: I once heard about a sales rep that brought out their computer and showed a deck at lunch. Not to show ideas or examples of work, but to roll through a general presentation. The client was so turned off by this move they vowed never to work with this person. The sales rep was more interested in their own property vs. hearing about the client's needs.

Oh, and a last tip to share re: casual meetings, be nice to your waiter. A smart client will watch how you interact with the waitstaff. Are you kind, do you critique your order, do you send back your order, and do you tip? They are paying attention, no doubt. Tip 20% (no matter what) and eat your dinner (no matter what). And if you're taking out the AMEX client, use an AMEX to pay for the meal. Don't be a fool and use your Discover. Clients are watching and these details matter. I once ordered a "small cappuccino" with the Starbucks client and they never forgot. I think about it every time I'm at a Starbucks - TALL Cappuccino please!

The last part of the meeting is crucial.
Don't walk out or hang up the phone until you have a next step.
Whether it's showing ideas, pricing out an existing offer, or even setting up a 2nd meeting, don't end the meeting without calling-out and identifying the next step and with the client agreeing.

You'll be sending a follow up email shortly (more on that in the coming pages), and you'll want to include your next step to take the conversation and opportunity to the next level.

If you walk out without identifying your next step, well…there just won't be one.

And a last thought when talking "meetings" – get to know the office receptionist and office assistants with your clients. They are your "in" to the office and without a doubt are sharing feedback about you to your clients. Know their name, be friendly, be positive – and thank them when you walk in AND out of the office. You may also want to send a thank you email post meeting directly to your client's assistant, as they more than likely coordinated schedules to fit you in.

You may even want to extend small gifts at holiday time. Nothing crazy expensive here, just thoughtful. It will go a long way.

Part #3 – The Follow Up

You've had your meeting, you gained a ton of valuable information on your client's needs, wishes, challenges and you even tossed out ideas, which may have resonated. As a past manager once said, "Can you smell that? Can you smell the money?"

There are three (3) things to do post meeting, and in this order:

1) Write that Call Report – exit the elevator, catch a cab, and flip on your hotspot – write that Call Report. You'll get the most thorough Call Report if you write it right away. Just 5 minutes max – jot down the notes from your mind and your notebook into the Call Report document. It does not need to be fancy or grammatically correct, just a "dump" of the knowledge you obtained. Once my notes are digital, I rip out the pages of my notebook and throw them away (I'm not a paper person). If there are action items you need to respond on, note them within the "Next Steps" section and if you need a team member's help with any items, highlight their name here so it's easy to see (and place a deadline). Send this Call Report in email to your manager, your marketing designee and sales planner. Sending the Call Report internally does a few things, 1) it provides timely updates on your business, so management knows what you're up to 2) enables the team to act fast as you'll be mapping out responsibilities in the "Next Step" section, and 3) and it shows your activity levels effectively. Rember, activity = selling.

2) Write Your Follow Up Note, then Send It – note, I said "write it," I did not say send it right away. Don't be "that rep" sending a follow up note 10 minutes after the meeting, but on the flip side, don't wait too long. I'd suggest sending a follow up note 4 – 24 hours post meeting. The more urgent the need, the quicker you send. Do not wait and send a follow up note days after a meeting. It's your job to be prompt and stay relevant with your client.

When you do send that Follow Up Note, similar to when you meet in person, do not write, "Thank you so much for taking the time to meet with me today." Instead, say, "It was so great to meet you today. Happy we were able to connect." You are equals. Include items you discussed, ideas shared, work you've created, and answers to any questions that were not addressed in the meeting itself.

3) Get Personal – getting personal is key with your client. I'm not talking about taking weekend getaways here or becoming BFFs, but there needs to be a personal connection, or a level of comfort with each other to share ideas/create the best partnership. Sprinkled throughout your meeting, you hope to gain/give information about each other. Be authentic and share true stories. When the client does open up and share personal information, keep track of it. It's gold.

Mark down this information in your contact excel sheet (while you're writing your Call Report). Such as, Rebecca is gluten free, John is getting married May 2021, Karen hates fruit in her salad, you name it. Remembering these sorts of things will set you apart from other sales reps. For example, the next time you bring in donuts to Rebecca's office, and you give her the gluten free one, she'll love it and really appreciate you remembering. These sorts of small details go a long way.

Also, after your meeting and after you've sent the Follow Up Note, connect with each person you met on LinkedIn. LinkedIn is a very powerful contact source for salespeople and growing your "network" on this platform it very important.

Splits 101: They're Inevitable

Yup, splits are inevitable, but when an account is shared among two sales reps, there's potential to play a powerful game of strategy.

So, what is a split?
When a client and their media agency are located in different territories, for example, Subaru is in NJ, Carmichael Lynch is in Minneapolis. This means, two reps in each market are covering the business and the commission is split among both reps. Before you work for a company, ask about the split policy so you know what you're walking into. I always side with, "if you do the work, you get the split, but just because the client is located in your territory, it doesn't mean you get a piece of the commission."

Two (2) things to know when creating a successful split partnership:
1) **Know the Players** – before you pursue a client, look up the account. Where's the client located? Where are the agencies located? Knowing beforehand if the business is a split will save you headaches down the road. If the account is a split, talk with your partner before pursuing. They may have useful intel to share with you.
2) **Share the Same Brain** - when intel is gained, share it with your split partner and in a timely fashion. Have an upcoming call with a client? Tell your partner. Work together to gain intel, leverage relationships and build the strongest partnership possible. You may even want to set up 1X month meetings/calls with your split partners to review account updates and talk strategies. Talk strategy on pulling in a piece of business.

Elevator Pitch: You have 3 Minutes...

Your elevator pitch. Have one…and be ready.

Yes, you need to know your GP (general presentation) for meetings, and such, but you also need to have your quick elevator pitch at the ready.

There are three (3) parts to your elevator pitch:

1) The first part is **your opener**, that one-liner you state when someone says, "what do you do? Or, where do you work?" Summarize your product in one statement – something people will automatically understand from the get-go. You'll use this one-liner at networking events, etc. as part of your introduction. And feel free to be punchy and clever. It will create intrigue.

2) Once you state your Opener, and you see there's intrigue, then follow it up with **more details** on your property. Quick facts, growth stats, where you're headed, etc.

3) Then, **ask for the meeting**. Say something like, "we've seen your work with XX, and we'd love to talk about ways we can help. Let's set up some time to talk – next week? Tuesday, 10am?"

Trust your instincts on when to say it, what to say, and how to close, but ultimately, you are looking to gain time to talk further.

Email Techniques:
Increase Your Response Rate

There are no full-proof "tricks" to getting people to respond to you in email, but there are things you can do to increase your chances.

1) **Be Direct** – state what you want right from the get-go at the top of the email. "Hi Greg, I want to meet you. Next Tuesday, 10am?"
2) **Provide Value** – give the client a reason to meet with you / a real benefit
3) **Reiterate What You Want** – at the close of the email, state again what you want
4) **"How are you?" or "How was your weekend?"** – do not ask these sorts of questions, and especially if you do not know the person directly. It's fluff and doesn't serve a purpose.

Cold Email Example:

Subject: Tuesday 1/15, 10am
Hi Greg, we want to meet you. Next Tuesday, 10am an option?
We've seen your work with XX and I'd love to learn more about this campaign approach for next year and the audience you're after. Here at COMPANY, we're the fastest growing digital media brand reaching XXX. We've worked with 100+ brands, creating ownable branded assets distributed across the COMPANY network. Here are some examples:
* *XXX (link out to work that is applicable to the client (their category, their competitor) and any awards it received - #4 viewed on FB, etc etc)*
* *XXX*

Hopeful Tuesday, 1/15 10am works for you.
Looking forward to it!
Allison

Often times, reps are always asking for something from clients in email. We want to meet, host a call, show you something, sell you something... Sometimes, send your key client's emails that have nothing to do with work. The holidays are a great time. Something like, "Hi Rebecca, just wanted to wish you a Happy Thanksgiving! Hope you have a wonderful time with your family." I learned this from a past manager, and these sorts of emails go a long way. Trust me.

Email Etiquette:
Common Sense Guidelines

A few guidelines to follow when it comes to emailing:

- **Respond Quickly** - a client emails you a question, a request, you name it…you respond immediately. "Let me look into this for you. I'll be in touch. Stay tuned!" You *may* also want to ask when they want this information, so you're in line with their timing needs. Never let an unanswered email from a client sit for more than 4 hours. Never.

- **"Thank you"** – never hit reply-all and say, "Thank you." Just hit reply and say "Thank you" to the person that helped you. Not everyone needs to see the pleasantries. We all get too much email as it is.

- **Post 4pm on a Friday** – do not email clients and agencies. Too late to start prospecting now. The work week is over.

- **Before 9am to an agency is a <u>NO</u>** – don't be that rep. Don't send a cold email to a media buyer before 9am. Go ahead and craft your emails before then and set them to a timer to be sent post 9am. If your email is a response to their question, then by all means, send.

- **Before 9am to a client or a C-Suite is a <u>YES and ALWAYS</u>** – executives start their day early, and really early. The best time to catch these guys/gals are on their way to work. No time is too early. And once they respond to your note, respond immediately back. It's likely, they are "free" and not in a meeting and you may have caught them at a good time to have a nice back/forth dialogue.

Grow Your Business:
Do These Three (3) Simple Things

---

1) **Grow Your Deal Size** – take a look at your average deal size from last year. Keep that number in your head and as you plan for the year ahead, ensure your future offerings are higher.

2) **Grow the Number of Deals** – Increasing the number of deals you close is also another way to increase your revenue. 1x per quarter, take a careful look at your territory and do a "new sweep" of who's in the marketplace. Maybe accounts moved, agencies moved, you name it. Always refresh your prospecting pool. Things move around constantly in this business. And speaking of prospecting....

   · Another good tip is to take a look at who is spending in print. These guys have to commit weeks/months ahead of time to make printing schedules, so if you see a brand in market in print, they may also be planning digital soon. Get on it!

   · Watch linear TV – who's getting behind storytelling that speaks to your brand? Who's targeting your demo? Once I see an ad, I email the client shortly thereafter (snag the link from ispot.tv) and say something like, *"Hey, I just saw your ad on XXX. Love it! We'd love to hear more about your strategy in reaching XXXX, as COMPANY XX is the fastest growing digital media brand reaching XXXX."* Brands that spend in TV have big bucks, and they're very comfortable in the video space as well.

   · Sift through sites such as BrandTale, SellerCrowd, Winmo, MediaRadar, AutoNews, etc and even listen to market Podcasts (my favorite is MarketSnacks Daily) to see who's spending and what they're up to. Always keep your eyes/

ears peeled for opportunities and reference how you heard about them.

3) **Grow What Your Existing Clients Spend with You** – it's always easier getting existing buyers to spend more with you vs onboarding a fresh, new partner. The existing clients know you and are comfortable with you, and if they like their partnership with you, will feel more comfortable putting money with you vs. a new publisher. Toward the end of the year, when management pushes you hardest to bring in last minute deals, always look to your existing clients first and offer them ways to plus up their existing partnership with you.

Negotiating

With a Potential Client

We could spend hours talking about this subject – the techniques, the strategies, the pace/flow, etc., but "learning how to negotiate" is truly something you get better at, with real life practice. You can spend hours reading business books on the subject, but really – it's a learned skill. All I can tell you…and I've said this before, is that closing deals is a lot like dating. If they like you, you will know. If they want to buy you, you will know.

Silence = not good.

If your offer is in true consideration, you're going to get questions, requests, and in a timely fashion. When it comes to negotiating and "holding onto" their interest in the program, it's all about achieving a "win-win." You want to get the deal in a place where your client feels good about it (they see their ROI, they see the value you bring to the deal), and you also want to craft a deal where you win – a deal that is profitable internally.

There is a component of standing your ground, not moving on price, especially if they truly like you/want to buy you, they'll find a way and find the money to put behind it. Negotiating is just a game of push and pull, and I've often found that the "let's meet in the middle" tactic works successfully. You want a $30CPM, they want a $20CPM – *"let's meet in the middle at $25 and move forward."*

With An Employer – Negotiating Your Pay

I've hosted conversations with many young executives on this subject, and it's without a doubt an arena where you'll need your community/ network to push you to the next level. Your connections can help you leverage intel to put yourself in the best position for a raise. You're able to talk out options, gain insights on where to push/what not to push, find out what's realistic, what's the "going rates" in the marketplace, and how to position yourself/decipher your points of differentiation.

Quick Tip - yes, yes, we've all heard it. Never take the first offer. Always ask for the "final and best," and be willing to walk away if the money isn't there. When you're negotiating your comp plan, take note of your approach. Potential employers are watching you. They want to see your self-positioning, and your style. After all, you'll take these negotiating tactics with you when working with potential partners.

Negotiating your pay in your 20s is very different from your 30s, 40s and 50s. The older you get, the more experience you have and value you bring to an organization, the more complicated your contracts are and having a lawyer review your documents can be supremely helpful.

Your Brand:
You will be judged.

You greet your client for the first time, you walk into a meeting, you say hello on a conference call, you will be judged. As we stated earlier, the first 3 seconds are crucial. Clients will be compartmentalizing you right from the get-go, so don't blow it.

Walk in with a smile on your face, excited to be there – and be authentic.

Clients can immediately tell if you're not your true self.

Find a way to "brand yourself" and set yourself apart from other sales reps. When I first moved to Chicago, the company I was representing had an awareness issue. Not everyone knew of it. I had to get our company's name and offerings out in the marketplace and in a vast/ notable way. The market also didn't know me, so I had to do the same for my own personal brand. So, I started bringing donuts to every meeting. I have a donut blog, so naturally, this was the easiest thing for me to do. I was being true to my own interests and it created a fantastic meeting opener. I even made "Best Donuts in Chicago" cards, mapping out my favorite spots for clients to try. It was a nice way to open cold/1st time meetings and I became known as the "donut lady." A title I love.

Know Your Audience

If you're walking into a room of clients that make $40k/year, don't rock your Givenchy bag and Prada shoes. Be respectful of the people you meet, and the dialogue you have.

And if you're meeting with the Lands' End client, wear Lands' End clothes.

I love me some Lands' End.

Also, the more corporate environment you're in, the more corporate you need to look.

The less corporate, you get it…

The only time you can bring out your designer digs?

When you are meeting with a designer client.

Know Everyone:
Top-Down, know everyone.

Networking, establishing your personal brand, and driving revenue – it's all centered around the people you know.

Knowing a C-level executive does a little for you, but it's really just the tip of the iceberg. C-Suites can tell you the next person to talk to, but they often times are not the ones signing contracts and closing deals. They certainly approve and are part of large partnership agreements but knowing just the CMO is not going to close the deal. You also sound like a d-bag when you say, "Oh, well, I know the CMO." No one cares. You need to know the ENTIRE team – office assistant, all the way up to the CMO/CEO. Expand too, to other divisions within the company. Know everyone.

As stated prior, it only takes one person to say NO to a deal for a potential partnership to fall apart. Your job is to get everyone on board with your property and share the value you can bring to their company.

Networking is essential.
Join industry groups and meet/interact with new people in your business. Don't just join these groups to add to your resume, but attend meetings, join a committee, help plan events and participate in networking events.

I just have one rule to abide by:
You've walked into a Holiday Happy Hour with an organization. You know no one. You only have one job to do: Meet One New Person. That's it. You do not need to talk/meet with the entire group, just one new person. Don't make this overwhelming. Make a connection, have a

conversation, trade business cards (if those still exist? Ha!) and connect with them on LinkedIn post event. Networking is an independent sport. It's all up to you on how you master it.

Internal Relations: Don't be a dick.

Management's worst nightmare:
An incredible salesperson, but they are an ass to their internal teams.
Don't be this guy/gal.

"Managing the perception of you" internally is as important as your outward-facing demeanor with clients. There's no way you can be a success without being a team-player inside your organization. You could sell the biggest deal of your life, but if your internal teams don't respect you, don't trust you, or you've set them up for failure when it comes to production/performance expectations, the deal will fall apart and more than likely, your clients will never come back - no matter where you work.

Open communication with all internal teams is essential.

As a deal moves from submitted, to Q/A, to verbal, you better have updated your internal teams, so they know status and what's expected when/if it moves to sold. When the deal officially closes, and you share all deal points/agreements/expectations with internal teams, be honest on all areas. If the client has different expectations, they will come to light with the execution teams.

Also, and very important, do not "hand off" the deal to your internal teams once it's sold and never look back. Your job as the company's representative is to ensure you are part of the execution and the client is happy. Be present on all pre-pro/execution calls and chime in on emails when necessary. Trust me, clients notice when you've "handed them off." It's not good.

Dos & Don'ts

Dos

- Always carry some sort of swag/gift – for that "just in case" moment with a client. I once represented a parenting brand, so I have a branded baby onesie in my bag just in case I have a client announcing their pregnant
- More so than not, *true* decision makers (those that make purchasing decisions/sign contracts) want to be entertained differently. Save the nights out boozing for the younger associates. True decision makers want early morning breakfasts, Cubs tickets (get great seats), and fun experiences (meditation rooms, bath houses, etc). Get creative with your offerings and ideas. The more creative, the bigger/positive response you'll get.
- You're on vacation – your natural instinct tells you to put on your out of office message. You include your manager as your back up, but really…are you unavailable? Again, sales is self-inflicted pain. If you want to close the deal, you'll chime in on the email, even on your vacation. Perhaps share a "status" with your manager before going out on leave so they can take the necessary steps to move your deal along while you're out.
- The more southern you are (Texas, Georgia, etc), start your meeting with pleasantries. Being raised in the South, I can tell you, southerners like to know you before doing business. If you jump right into the work, they won't want to work with you.
- Get in trouble with a client. Maybe you emailed too many times, or too often…this is good. You'll never "get in trouble" with management if a client is upset for you reaching out too much. You're smart. You'll soon learn the right cadence for your clients. It takes patience and practice.

Don'ts

- Don't ever say, "I have the perfect idea for you." You have no idea what's perfect for them. Let them say it's perfect. Not you.
- When you're waiting to hear if you've made the buy, don't say "fingers crossed." Instead, really think through all of the players/decision makers, your ideas, your pricing...have you *really* done everything you can to close the deal? Crossing your fingers will do nothing for you.
- Never count your money. You've just received a contract and you begin to work the math in your head as far as commission. Then, you start adding up all of the deals you'll be paid on this quarter. It's bad luck. Don't count your money before it's in your bank account. Instead, take this time to close another deal.
- No need to apologize – this is business, not personal. You screwed up on something? Just fix it and move on. No need to apologize.
- "How's the weather?" No. No. Do not ask this question on a conference call as you wait for others to join, or in your pursuit to make a connection. It's filler and no one really cares or wants to talk about how cold it is.
- When you're interviewing for a job, don't ask, "what are the hours?" That's a clear sign you have no idea what sales means. When you are selling, you are always working. There are no hours. You make your own hours.

Last Words

Hopeful you will use this little black book as a guide as you navigate the fun world of sales. I have found sales to be an incredible practice, especially for young women. The flexibility with schedules (you can actually make that 2pm event at your daughter's school), the opportunity to make money and ultimately pay for your daughter's college, and the creativity in finding the right partnership with a partner. I love it!

I know I have said this repeatedly, that "sales is self-inflicted pain," so it is up to you to determine your own success.

No one is going to just "give you" money.

You have got to fight your way in and define your points of differentiation for a buyer. Make their job easy and position your offerings as the "no brainer" solution.

To sell a partnership is tough these days, and nothing is a "must buy" anymore. Clients are looking more closely at their investments and the value they gain from their partnerships. With all the hard work you will put into this career, at the end of the day, do one thing >> ask for the business. Ask for the money! Express your interest in working with them…and close the deal.

Allison McEntee is a visionary marketer whose creativity and entrepreneurialism have expanded business, increased revenue and scaled partnerships. Deep experience in developing successful partnerships with Fortune 500 clients, from ideation to execution. Background includes broadcast sales and buying, integrated marketing, digital content and e-commerce-led initiatives. Allison is also incredibly passionate about her Brand Ambassador and Leadership Development Committee Chair roles with She Runs It, an organization paving the way for women to lead at every level in marketing and media.

Allison currently lives in a John Hughes film in a suburb on the northside of Chicago with her incredible husband and awesome three kids.